W9-BKL-577

Randall McDaniel

by Mark Stewart

ACKNOWLEDGMENTS
The editors wish to thank Randall McDaniel for his cooperation in preparing this book.
Thanks also to Integrated Sports International for their assistance.

PHOTO CREDITS
All photos courtesy AP/Wide World Photos, Inc. except the following:

Sports Chrome – Cover, 24 bottom left
Michael F. Corrado/Sports Chrome – 2 top, 45
Mark Brettingen – 5 top, 5 bottom right, 6, 22, 24 bottom right, 25, 28, 29, 30 top, 31, 35, 38, 39, 40, 41
Randall McDaniel – 4 center right, 4 bottom right, 8, 9, 10, 11, 12, 13, 15, 32, 33, 43 top right, 43 bottom left
Arizona State University – 16, 17, 18, 19, 24 top, 26
Minnesota Vikings – 42, 43 top left, 43 bottom right
Sports Media, Inc. – 27
Mark Stewart – 48

STAFF
Project Coordinator: John Sammis, Cronopio Publishing
Series Design Concept: The Sloan Group
Design and Electronic Page Makeup: Jaffe Enterprises, and
        Digital Communications Services, Inc.

LIBRARY OF CONGRESS CATALOGING-IN-PUBLICATION DATA
Stewart, Mark.
    Randall McDaniel / by Mark Stewart.
        p. cm. – (Grolier all-pro biographies)
    Includes index.
    Summary: A brief biography of the Minnesota Vikings offensive lineman.
    ISBN 0-516-20180-8 (lib. bdg.) — 0-516-26028-6 (pbk.)
    1. McDaniel, Randall, 1964-   – Juvenile literature. 2. Football players—United States—
Biography—Juvenile literature. 3. Minnesota Vikings (Football team)—Juvenile literature.
[1. McDaniel, Randall, 1964-   . 2. Football players. 3. Afro-Americans—Biography.]
I. Title. II. Series.
GV939.M299S84 1996
796.332'092—dc20
(B)   96-1514
                                                                                                        CIP
                                                                                                        AC

©1996 Children's Press®, a Division of Grolier Publishing Co., Inc. All rights reserved.
Published simultaneously in Canada. Printed in the United States of America.
1 2 3 4 5 6 7 8 9 10 R 05 04 03 02 01 00 99 98 97 96

Grolier **ALL-PRO** *Biographies*™

Randall **McDaniel**

by
Mark Stewart

FLINT RIVER REGIONAL LIBRARY

CHILDREN'S PRESS®
A Division of Grolier Publishing
New York • London • Hong Kong • Sydney
Danbury, Connecticut

Contents

J   921.000 MCDANIE
STEWART, MARK
RANDALL MCDANIEL
1996
$20.00 PT 187935 C.05

NoLcx 11/12

Peachtree City Library
201 Willowbend Road
Peachtree City, Ga. 30269

Who

Am I?

In my family, I was the athlete and my brother was the brain. I never thought of myself as being smart. Fortunately, others believed in me when I did not. Because of that, I was able to build the confidence I needed to achieve my goal of becoming a professional athlete. My name is Randall McDaniel, and this is my story . . . "

"I was able to build the confidence I needed."

Randall McDaniel 64

Growing Up

Randall McDaniel grew up in the town of Avondale, Arizona, which is about an hour west of Phoenix. Because it is typically warm in the Southwest, Randall, his brother, and his three sisters could play outside almost every day of the year. Randall was big for his age, but he was very shy. One way he learned to meet other children was by participating in sports such as basketball, baseball, and football.

Randall and his best buddy, Glenn Rogers, spent practically all of their time together—playing games, going to the video arcade, or just hanging out and talking. Randall learned the importance of having someone he could count on, and it made him feel good to know that someone could count on him, too.

Six-year-old Randall McDaniel, when he was in the first grade

"If you have one good friend, you can face all the pressures of growing up much easier. Glenn and I were always there for each other." As he would discover many years later, being a good offensive lineman in football required the same kind of trust and support. Randall and Glenn were joined by a third boy, George Batts, and these "Three Musketeers" remained close friends through high school and college.

Randall was like a lot of kids in school. He loved to do fun science experiments, but there were some subjects he did not like at all. Randall found math was his most difficult subject. In fact, by the third grade, he thought he might never understand it. Part of the problem was that Randall liked to act tough and pretend he did not need help. But his teacher that year, Mrs. Pyle, saw a kid who just needed some kind words and a little self-confidence. She spent extra time with Randall and let him know that it was all right if he did not understand something right away. Then, once Randall got the hang of math, Mrs. Pyle made sure he kept up with the class.

Randall always enjoyed reading, especially when the books were about African-American heroes such as

Randall (right) with sisters Brenda and Nickel, and brother Kerry

At age eight, Randall joined his first baseball team.

Randall (left) and brother Kerry display their Little League trophies.

Frederick Douglass, Jackie Robinson, and Martin Luther King. Through elementary school, junior high, and high school, Randall stayed on top of his studies and learned that hard work was the key to achieving his goals. "Reading is the single most important thing to learn. It unlocks the world to a lifetime of discovery. If you can read, you can do anything. Because of the patience and love that Mrs. Pyle gave me in the classroom, I learned that I wasn't stupid. She was so important in making me who I am today—she believed in me and taught me to believe in myself. After that, whenever things got difficult, I always thought back to Mrs. Pyle and her belief in me. I owe a lot of my success to her."

Randall lived in a neighborhood where most of the families were either African-American or Hispanic. Sometimes he and his friends would visit the nearby town of Litchfield, where

The McDaniel brothers prepare for a musical career.

many white families lived. Some people in Litchfield objected to kids from Avondale using their playgrounds and parks, and on several occasions Randall and his friends were told to go home. Years later, when Randall became a high-school athlete, many of the kids who had not wanted him to play in their community became his teammates in football, basketball, and track. As he got to know these boys—and as they got to know him—they all realized that they had a great deal in common. For Randall, this understanding and togetherness was one of his favorite things about playing sports.

Randall played tight end and linebacker for Agua Fria High School in Avondale. At 6' 3" he was the biggest player on the team, and by his junior year he was one of the

As a high-school senior, Randall was an excellent all-around athlete. He starred in basketball and baseball as well as football.

Randall made more than 200 tackles playing high-school football.

best players in the entire Southwest. In all, Randall made more than 200 tackles in his high-school career. He also averaged more than 28 yards per catch as a receiver in his senior year. When college scouts first came to watch him play, they were impressed with his size and strength. But it was Randall's quickness and coordination as a blocker that convinced them he had a chance to become an All-American. After considering many scholarship offers, he chose to attend Arizona State University in the city of Tempe, less than 50 miles away.

When he was young, Randall's favorite player was Kellen Winslow, who played tight end for the San Diego Chargers. Randall admires Winslow even more today for his belief that athletes have a responsibility to be role models for the kids in their communities. Randall also admired Art Shell of the Oakland Raiders, whom he still considers "the best example of what an offensive lineman should be."

Randall's father, Robert, has been working as a bus driver and groundskeeper for the Litchfield School District for many years. His mother, Lela, stayed home and raised her five children. They taught their kids right from wrong. They told their children always to think a situation through and then do the right thing. As a result, none of the McDaniel children ever got into serious trouble.

"I handled the pressures of drugs and alcohol by hanging out with friends who didn't use them. Together, it was much easier to do our own thing. Also, I was kind of a bully, so people were a little scared of what I might do if I saw them experimenting with drugs or alcohol around me!"

Randall's high-school graduation ceremony

College

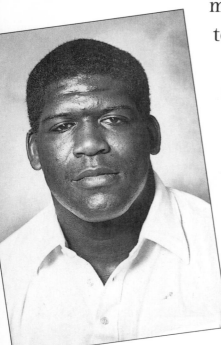

Randall McDaniel intended to play tight end for the Arizona State Sun Devils when he arrived in the fall of 1983, but the team was already loaded at that position. The decision was made to "red-shirt" him for a year. That meant he could practice with the team, but he was not eligible to play in games. Randall did not like this idea, but he understood that it might give him an extra season or two as a starter, beginning in 1984. In the meantime, Randall went to class and continued to build his body in the weight room.

When the 1984 season finally rolled around, however, there was a change of plans. Impressed by his quick feet and added muscle, the Arizona State coaches decided he might make a good offensive lineman. Randall agreed to switch, hoping that it would lead to

Before switching to offensive guard, Randall was "red-shirted" for a year.

Years

Randall's ability to pull out on a sweep made him an offensive force.

more playing time. After only eight days of practice at the guard position, he worked his way into the starting lineup! The Sun Devils were a good running team, but Randall made them even better with his ability to pull off the line and deliver crushing blocks. He was so fast for his size that he sometimes lined up in the backfield as a blocking back.

Randall's junior year (1986–87) was his favorite. The team won the PAC 10 championship and defeated the University of Michigan in the Rose Bowl. At season's end, the Sun Devils were ranked among the top five teams in the nation. For his part, Randall was an honorable mention All-American. In 1987–88, the team was nearly as good, finishing in the Top 20 and beating

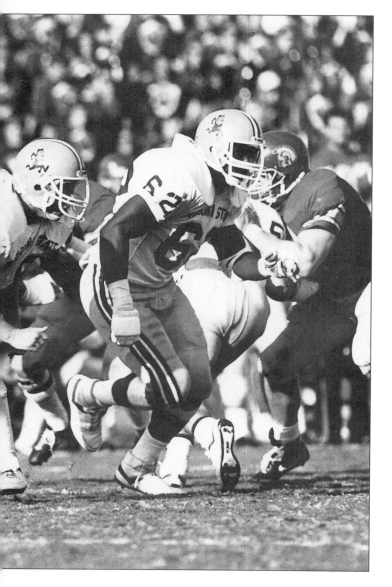

In his junior year, Randall led Arizona State to the Freedom Bowl.

the Air Force Academy in the Freedom Bowl. One of the highlights of that season was that Randall's younger brother, Kerry, made the team.

Randall graduated in the spring of 1988 with a degree in physical education. There was no doubt in anyone's mind that he would be a first-round pick in the NFL draft.

Randall's work in the weight room helped him on the field and also earned him national recognition off the field. In 1986, he was the American Drug-Free Powerlifting Association's collegiate champion in the 275-pound weight division. He also set a college record by deadlifting 620 pounds.

Randall remembers college fondly. "The school experience taught me as much about life as any subject did. I learned to be responsible for my actions, and that you have to be true to yourself. I also learned what true friendship is and how important it is in life.

"Winning the 1987 Rose Bowl over Michigan has been my most satisfying football moment. We had the best offensive line in the nation that year, and we were all Arizona kids. It was the perfect ending to a great season."

The Story

While Randall McDaniel was doing great things on the college football field, the Minnesota Vikings were thinking about how nice it would be to have a big, mobile player on their front line. After 18 players were selected in the 1988 NFL draft, the Vikings were delighted to find that Randall was still available, and they made him their first-round pick. Randall was thrilled to be chosen by the Vikings, but he was shocked that he would have to move from the warmest part of the country to the coldest!

An injury to Minnesota's first-string guard gave Randall a chance to play in the second game of the season. Randall made the most of this opportunity and won the

At the 1988 NFL draft, Randall was the 19th pick in the first round.

starting job. His pass blocking helped Wade Wilson lead the league in completion percentage.

By his second pro season, Randall was considered one of the top linemen in the game. Realizing what a talented young blocker they had, the Vikings decided they needed a superstar to run behind him. The team made a monster trade, sending several young players and future draft choices to the rebuilding Dallas Cowboys in exchange for Herschel Walker, who had gained 1,514 yards the year before.

When the Vikings traded for Herschel Walker (right), Randall had an All-Pro running back to block for.

At first, the trade helped the Vikings, who won the Central Division title. But in the long run, it proved to be a disaster. Without good, young players to replace the old and injured, Minnesota dropped to 6–10 in 1990 and finished a mediocre 8–8 in 1991. Still, Randall played brilliantly, earning All-Pro recognition both years.

The team's fortunes began to turn around in 1992, when Dennis Green was hired to run the team. His plan was to build around talented stars like Randall and make full

Randall was named All-Pro again in 1994.

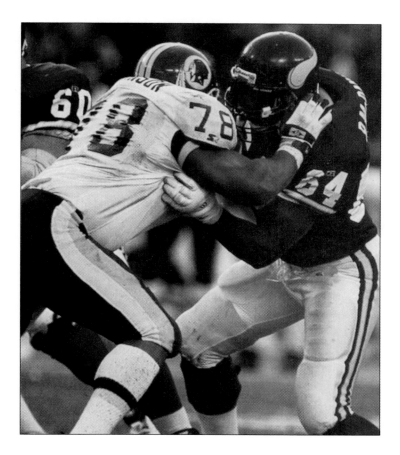

Randall is the top offensive lineman in Minnesota Vikings history.

use of their abilities. By the end of Green's first season, the Vikings were division champs again with an impressive 11–5 record. And Randall was honored once more as the best at his position.

By 1995, Randall had established himself as the top offensive lineman in team history. No other Viking has been voted All-Pro more often, and only defensive tackle Alan Page has played in more Pro Bowls.

"I have worked very hard to make sure that no part of my game—physically or mentally—is a weak spot."

Timeline

1987: Helps Arizona State beat Michigan in the Rose Bowl

1989: Earns All-Pro honors in second NFL season

1988: Joins NFL Minnesota Vikings and wins starting job in second game

1996: Plays in his seventh straight Pro Bowl

1992: Has one of his finest years under new coach Dennis Green

1994: Helps Minnesota Vikings win their third division title in six years

Game

Randall wore uniform number 88 in high school and became number 62 when he moved to guard at Arizona State. "Today, I wear number 64. That's the year I was born!"

How good was Randall in college? He gave up only one sack during his four years at Arizona State!

Action!

Randall has lined up at fullback for the Vikings on several occasions. Although he has never carried the ball, he has delivered key blocks in crucial goal-line situations.

Randall believes he is still a player on the rise. "I can still get better. I'm looking for that 100 percent perfect game."

andall says, "I am very proud of the fact that I have become the 'complete package' at my position."

"I try to know my opponent's strengths and weaknesses and use them against him. I try to get inside his head."

Randall is a tremendous drive-blocker for his size. His ability to move defenders backward opens up huge holes for Vikings running backs.

Playing offensive line is like being in a fight.

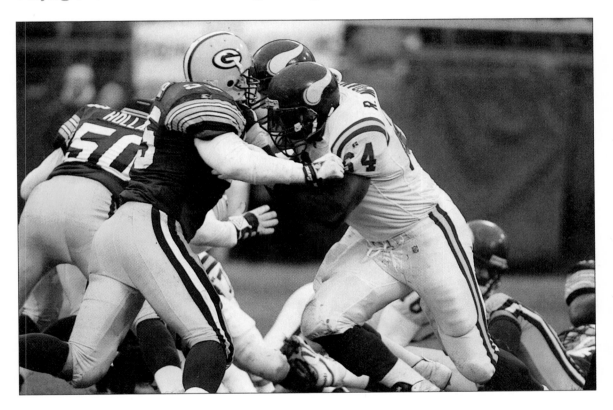

Everyone knew McDaniel would be an All-Pro performer during his standout rookie year. Most NFL guards do not even start until their second or third seasons.

Dealing

Responsibilities and expectations—for Randall McDaniel, these two aspects of being a professional athlete are the toughest to deal with. He knows what he would like to accomplish during and after his playing days, but sometimes people expect much more.

Randall devotes many hours to children in the Twin Cities area.

With It

"I believe it is my role to use the opportunity football is giving me to make a difference in the lives of kids. But it is often hard to be all things to all people."

Randall also works with the Minnesota Vikings to help kids. The Viking Children's Fund raises millions of dollars for child-related organizations. Randall also works at the NFL Coca-Cola/McDonald's Mini Camp for Kids. The free camp, held where the Vikings practice, gives kids a chance to learn lessons about life and football.

Randall tutors a young offensive lineman-to-be.

How Does

R andall McDaniel ranks among the best pulling guards ever to play in the NFL. He is fast enough to "pull" back off the line of scrimmage and sprint to the outside, where he can open a huge hole for the running back. The secret is not in Randall's size . . . it's in his shoes!

"I try to combine my speed and strength with good footwork. That's what makes me a successful offensive guard."

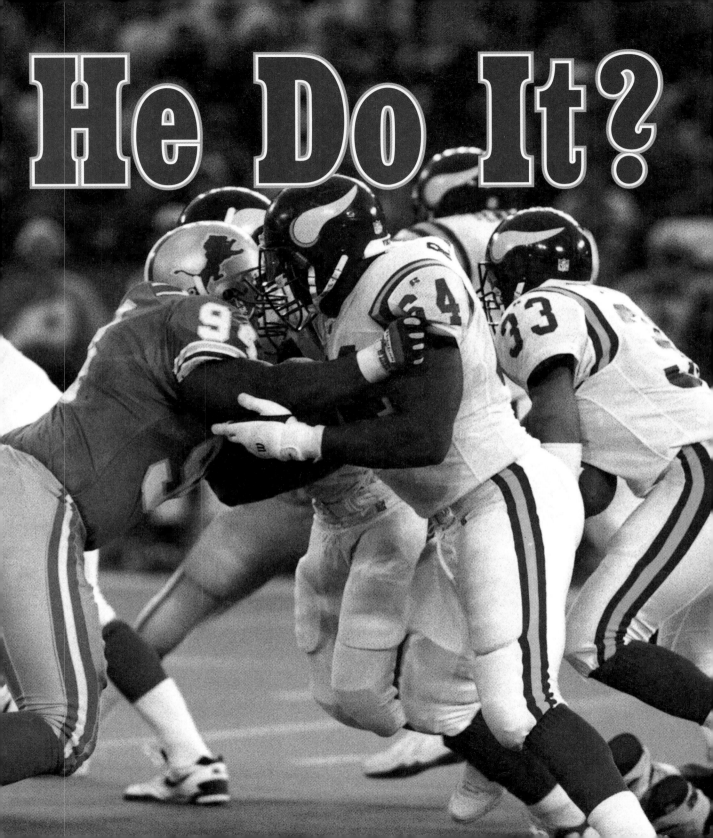

He Do It?

Say What?

Here's what football people are saying about Randall McDaniel:

"Randall plays hard and plays smart."

—*Dennis Green,*
  Minnesota Vikings head coach

"Randall could be one of the five best guards ever to play the game."

—*Dave Huffman, former teammate*

"Randall's an excellent athlete, and he's got the right mental attitude."

—*John Michels,*
former Vikings offensive line coach

"He's not a regular athlete, but he's a regular guy."

—*Brian Habib, former teammate*

"He's everything a number-one draft pick is supposed to be."

—*Gene McGivern, sportswriter*

"Randall's a great Pro Bowl player who boosts everyone around him."

—*Todd Steussie,*
Minnesota Vikings tackle

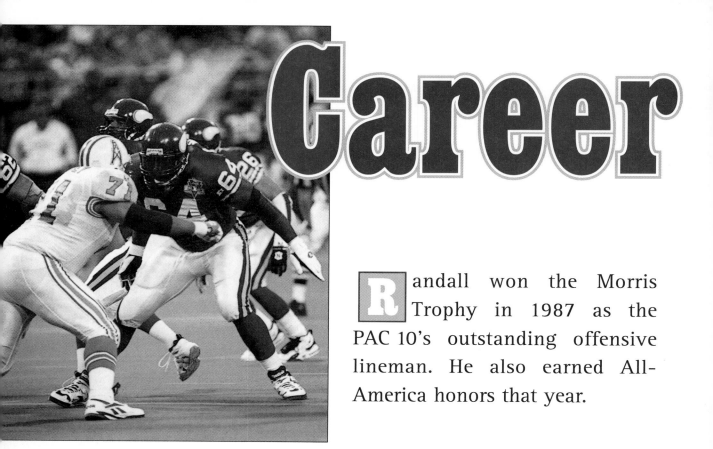

Career

andall won the Morris Trophy in 1987 as the PAC 10's outstanding offensive lineman. He also earned All-America honors that year.

Randall played in several college all-star games, including the Japan Bowl, Senior Bowl, and East-West Shrine Game.

When the Vikings selected Randall with the 19th overall pick in the 1988 NFL draft, it marked the first time since 1964 that the team had chosen an offensive lineman in the first round.

Highlights

The Vikings racked up an NFC-best 2,201 rushing yards behind Randall in 1991.

Randall was named to the NFL All-Rookie team in 1988. His 15 starts at guard that season were the most ever by a Vikings rookie.

Randall's seventh straight Pro Bowl appearance in 1996 tied him with all-time great Ron Yary for the most by a Minnesota offensive lineman.

In 1996, Randall became only the second seven-time All-Pro in Minnesota Vikings history.

Reaching

Nothing makes Randall McDaniel sadder than the thought of a child who cannot read. That is why he puts in countless hours at local elementary schools, trying to reach out to kids who need help with their reading skills. Sometimes, Randall brings a teammate along. The players love it because it gives them a chance to make a difference in a young person's life.

"Sometimes young boys think reading is sissy. I try to prove them wrong!"

At a YMCA, Randall takes over the reading chores.

Out

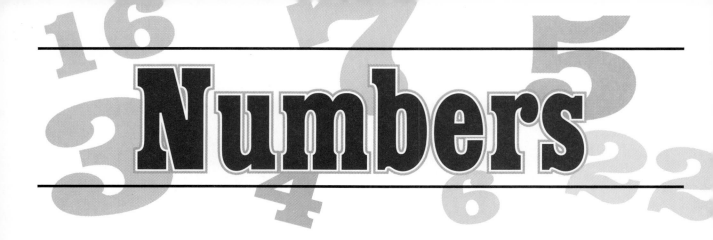

Numbers

Name: Randall Cornell McDaniel

Born: December 19, 1964

Height: 6' 3"

Weight: 275 pounds

Uniform Number: 64

College: Arizona State University

The Vikings have had only one losing season since Randall joined the team in 1988. From 1989 to 1994, they won the NFC Central Division title three times.

Year	Team	Games	Team Record	Division Rank	Team Rushing Yards	Division Rank
1988	Minnesota Vikings	16	11-5	2	1,806	2
1989	Minnesota Vikings	14	10-6	1	2,066	2
1990	Minnesota Vikings	14	6-10	5	1,867	3
1991	Minnesota Vikings	16	8-8	3	2,201	1
1992	Minnesota Vikings	16	11-5	1	2,030	1
1993	Minnesota Vikings	16	9-7	2	1,623	3
1994	Minnesota Vikings	16	10-6	1	1,524	4
1995	Minnesota Vikings	16	8-8	4	1,733	3

What If...

When I first came to the NFL, my goal was to play ten years, which is much longer than the average lineman lasts. Luckily, it looks as if I might make it. What might I have done if things didn't work out so well? I would be doing the same thing that I plan to do after I retire: teaching elementary school. The courses I studied in college gave me a good foundation to go back and get my teaching credentials. And all these years I've been working with school kids has really convinced me that this is what I should be doing with my life."

Glossary

CONFIDENCE a feeling of trust and belief in oneself

CREDENTIALS proof of having knowledge in a certain area, such as a diploma or a certificate

BESTOWED given; presented to

COMPLEXITIES the hard-to-understand parts; the difficulties

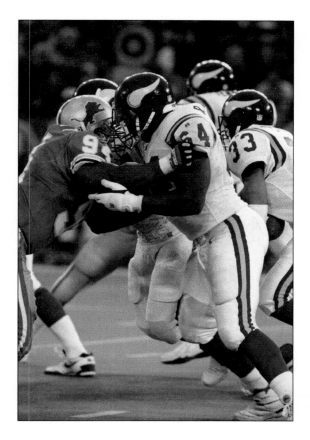

MOBILE able to move
about freely

RETIRE to stop working at
a job

REQUIRED called for;
necessary

SCHOLARSHIP money given
to a student to help pay
for schooling

TRIBUTE a demonstration of
respect; a show of gratitude

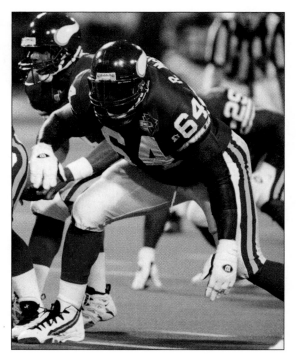

CRUCIAL very important;
significant

ELIGIBLE possessing the
abilities needed to perform
a task

IMPACT a strong,
immediate effect

MEDIOCRE so-so; average;
ordinary

Index

About The Author

Mark Stewart grew up in New York City in the 1960s and 1970s—when the Mets, Jets, and Knicks all had championship teams. As a child, Mark read everything about sports he could lay his hands on. Today, he is one of the busiest sportswriters around. Since 1990, he has written close to 500 sports stories for kids, including profiles on more than 200 athletes, past and present. A graduate of Duke University, Mark served as senior editor of *Racquet*, a national tennis magazine, and was managing editor of *Super News*, a sporting goods industry newspaper. He is the author of every Grolier All-Pro Biography.

Peachtree City Library
201 Willowbend Road
Peachtree City, Ga. 30269